VANISHING AFRICA

VANISHING AFRICA

Photographs, Text and Layout by
Leni Riefenstahl

Translated from the German by Kathrine Talbot

Harmony Books/New York

Published by Harmony Books, a division of Crown Publishers, Inc.,
One Park Avenue, New York, New York 10016 and simultaneously
in Canada by General Publishing Company Limited   ·

HARMONY BOOKS and colophon are trademarks of Crown
Publishers, Inc.

Manufactured in Italy by Arnoldo Mondadori Editore, Verona

Library of Congress Cataloging in Publication Data

Riefenstahl, Leni.
   Vanishing Africa.

   1. Africa, Eastern—Description and travel—Views.
2. Ethnology—Africa, Eastern—Pictorial works. I. Title.
DT365.19.R53 1982   779′.99676   82-11835
ISBN 0-517-54914-X

10 9 8 7 6 5 4 3 2 1

First American Edition

CONTENTS

About the Photographs

The photographs in this book were taken with the following 35 mm cameras: Leica M2, Leica M3 and Leica M5, and with the following reflex cameras: Leicaflex SL Mot and Leica R3 Mot.

Except for the Nuba of Kau and the animal photos I generally used the Leica M2 and Leica M3. On the whole I used normal lenses, between 35 and 90 mm. But for the Nuba of Kau and the animal photographs I had to use a telephoto lens – because it isn't always possible to get close to the animals, and because the Nuba of Kau, unlike the Mesakin Nuba, were very shy. In these cases I used telephoto lenses with focal lengths between 135 mm and 560 mm. Except for the moon pictures I never used a tripod. Instead, with very long focal lengths – 400 to 560 mm – I steady myself against a tree or wall, and support the lens with my left arm. I use a flash only for night-time photography and occasionally for contre-jour portraits.

I use Agfa CT 18, Agfachrome 50 S, Kodachrome, Kodak Ektachrome X and 64, and Ektachrome Highspeed film. In order to protect film against heat, which was essential — particularly in the Sudan, where we had night-time temperatures of over 40° Centigrade – I got the Africans to dig 3-metre trenches and line them with double layers of tarpaulin and earth. Miraculously, not a single film was spoiled. The temperature below ground was 34° Centigrade, maximum.

PREFACE

Africa means more to me than any other country. It has become my second home. I shall be homesick for Africa, its people, its animals, the deserts and savannahs as long as I live.

One of my first expeditions to Africa proved the most unusual. It took me ten months to travel from Khartoum to Nairobi. This was during 1962/63. I flew to Khartoum at the beginning of November and returned the following August. During this time I tramped through Africa, most of the time without a car or a tent, and with very little money. I joined a German expedition, but only for the first two months, after that I had to rely on myself. During the whole of this time I slept out of doors, mostly under trees. I had bought myself a light camp-bed in Khartoum, and I had a water canister and filter, a spirit stove and cooking pot, enough matches, a torch and batteries, a washbasin, eating implements, medicines and, of course, my Leica with films and flash equipment. My main provisions consisted of tea, sugar, powdered milk and porridge oats.

After I left the German group in Malakal in southern Sudan, My only transport, with one exception, were lifts on Arab trucks. I sometimes had to wait for weeks before a truck, usually loaded with cotton or salt, was able to take me on my way, sometimes only 50 kilometres, sometimes a hundred or even two hundred. I tried to spend the night near native huts most of the time. I had hardly put up my bed under a tree and made tea when, almost invariably, an audience began to appear. The mothers and children were usually the first, but sometimes the older men were even quicker off the mark. The girls and young men were shy, and it took days before I was able to get to know and photograph them.

I am often asked whether I wasn't afraid to be so completely alone in the African bush and to live among black people whom I did not know. My reply is that I have not felt as safe anywhere in Europe as I did during my solitary travels in Africa. I often met dark figures at night whom I did not recognise until they were a few yards from me. I was never threatened or molested. This too is part of the great magic that Africa has for me – being able to move about without fear.

I must add that my experience is chiefly of the Sudan, and may not apply to all African countries. And perhaps I had a good fairy looking after me. Who knows?

Ernest Hemingway
wrote in his book
GREEN HILLS OF AFRICA

'All I wanted to do now was get back to Africa. We had not left it, yet, but when I would wake in the night I would lie, listening, homesick for it already.'

Overleaf: – Leni Riefenstahl in Tanzania, East Africa, at the edge of the Ngorongoro crater.

CHAD

SUDAN

Nile

Port Sudan

RED SEA

N

Khartoum

White Nile

Blue Nile

FALATA NOMADS

El Obeid

Kadugli

NUBA
Kau

MESAKIN NUBA

SHILLUK

Malakal

NUER

ETHIOPIA

CENTRAL AFRICAN
REPUBLIC

Wau

DINKA

MURLE

Juba

Torit
LATUKA

ZAIRE

SAMBURU

KENYA

Equator

Mt Kenya
5199m

Lake
Victoria

Nairobi

RUANDA

MAASAI

Mt Kilimanjaro
5895m

BURUNDI

Arusha

Mombasa

INDIA

OCEA

TANZANIA

Dar-es-Salaam

0   400   800 km

Introduction:

MY BELOVED AFRICA

On April 5th 1956 I was shivering in wet and cold weather at Frankfurt airport, waiting for my plane to take me to Khartoum, to Africa where I had never been, where I knew no-one, a totally strange continent. I had no idea at that moment that my encounter with Africa would completely change my life.

My departure for Africa was brought about by little more than chance. I had been reading Hemingway's *Green Hills of Africa*, a book which made a deep impression on me and which woke in me a longing to go to Africa. But my finances did not at that time stretch to such a journey. Then chance intervened. A few days after reading the book I received from a friend an unexpected few thousand Marks which I had lent him some time previously. I immediately decided to buy a ticket to fly to East Africa.

During the flight my life passed before my eyes like a film. My feelings were in turmoil and I could not sleep. The night seemed endless. Time and again I stared at the dark windows of the aeroplane. Then suddenly, miraculously there was colour. First the black of the night became transparent, then, within seconds, the most delicate colour appeared, changing from deepest blue to a floating light blue, from glassy green to a breath of pale yellow, from radiant orange to fiery red. And amongst all the colours swam the stars and above them hung, like embossed silver, the crescent of the southern moon. It was like an ocean of light, unbelievably clear and transparent in the colours of Paul Klee.

We were flying above the Sahara, the wings of the Super-Constellation vibrated, there was the muffled drone of the propellers. My first morning in Africa had begun.

We landed in Khartoum at sunrise. The damp cold of the murky German April still clung to my body. When I stepped out of the aeroplane I felt as if I were stepping into a bath of warm air. Enlarged by the haze and fine sand-dust, a gigantic sun stood above the airfield. The warm air met me and embraced my body. I was in a kind of trance from the moment I stepped on to the tarmac. I felt intoxicated, yet aware of everything.

In the fifty-four years of my life my world had been the mountains, the ice of Greenland, the lakes surrounded by reeds of the Mark Brandenburg, metropolitan Berlin. Here was something quite different, a new life was beginning. With the light behind them I saw the first black people I had seen for twenty years, since the Olympic Games of 1936 where I had watched the incredible grace and strength of Jesse Owens whom I had filmed again and again.

They seemed to float on a cushion of warm air, enlarged by the damp morning air, appearing detached from the earth like a mirage. They moved in slow motion, the sun behind them. The black faces, swathed in white cloths, the relaxed, walking figures, their wide robes blowing about them, moved towards me as in a profound dream – Africa had drawn me into a vision of beauty, strangeness and freedom.

It was to remain with me and affect me like a drug, and its dazing effect has not left me to this day although I have come to know the dark sides of African life and its seemingly almost insoluble social problems.

A few hours after that stop-over in Khartoum I was in Nairobi, my two old Leicas slung over my shoulder, planning the film on which I was pinning all my hopes, *Black Cargo*, a film about the contemporary slave trade. We went in a landrover to search for ideas for the film. George Six, the director of a safari company, who had been captain of the English swimming team at the Berlin Olympics, accompanied me.

Our first destination was the Tana River, a large river which flows into the Indian Ocean about 170 kilometres north of the equator near the Lamu peninsula. The landscape changed quickly, became sandy, the trees disappeared. The road led through silvery thorn-brush, no people or animals anywhere. A great emptiness greeted us, but there was something incredibly liberating about this solitude. I was overcome by a feeling of happiness such as I had never known before. The road along which we drove was closed to all vehicles during the rainy season, but George Six had a special permit.

It was at that moment of happiness and peace that it happened. A dwarf antelope jumped from the undergrowth to run across the road, George Six tore the steering wheel round, the car skidded in the deep red sand, the speedometer showed we were doing fifty miles an hour, speeding towards the two large corner-stones of a bridge.

My heart stopped. The front left wheel touched one of the

14

stones, the car was flung into the air, my head went through the windscreen, and the last thing I saw was that we were falling into a dry riverbed. Then I fainted.

Nobody used this closed road except the British District Officer who, once a month, inspected the African police station at Gorissa. On his trip back to Nairobi he stopped on a small bridge fifty kilometres south of Gorissa and, a few hours after our accident, noticed our overturned vehicle. The car lay on its back like a beetle, the wheels pointing to the sky. George Six and I were still unconscious, our bodies jammed under the car, half in and half out. Our heads and trunks which had gone through the windscreen were outside. The local boy who had accompanied us was jammed between boxes like a captive bird. A frightful pain woke me for a moment, and I became conscious of people trying to extricate me from the truck, then I sank back into unconsciousness coming to only because I felt myself being violently shaken. I noticed that I was lying on a vehicle which was moving and which was jerking me about most painfully. The pain was unbearable, and I fainted again. I don't know how long this journey lasted. What stays in my memory is that whenever I regained consciousness for a moment I thought of my mother whom I loved above all else. I also remember that I never felt that I was in serious danger. It was as if the drug of Africa was working.

I was lifted from the vehicle, heard voices, then I was carried into a room in which I recognised nothing in my half-conscious state.

I only learned much later what had happened. I had been taken to the Gorissa police station since I could not have survived the long journey to Nairobi. There was neither a doctor nor any medicines in Gorissa, just one syringe of morphine which was kept for the time when I was to be moved. George Six, who had been an auxiliary medical orderly in London during the war, sewed up the gaping wound in my scalp from which a large piece of blood-vessel was protruding, using a large darning needle and without an anaesthetic. Six's injuries were relatively minor. His kneecap was fractured, and he put his leg into splints himself. The boy was unhurt.

We had to wait at Gorissa for four days before a one-engine sports-plane which could take two people arrived, summoned by police radio. I was wrapped in a sheet and carried to the plane after Six had given me the morphine injection, which mercifully relieved me of the awful pain. The injection worked so quickly that I immediately lost all consciousness.

I was taken to the hospital in Nairobi where I lay in a room where the dying were housed. The medical superintendent, an Englishman, Professor Cohn, and his colleagues had, after examining me and looking at my X-rays, given up hope of my recovery. When I awoke from long hours of unconsciousness, it was so dark that I could not make out the objects around me.

My first feeling was one of happiness for I knew that I had survived the accident. I wanted to attract attention, but I could neither move nor make a sound. Hours passed before a figure entered the room. A little light came through the open door. It was a nurse who was leaning over some of the other beds, then noticed me. When she saw that my eyes were open she stood petrified. I tried to sit up but could do nothing. The effort made me lose consciousness again.

When I awoke once more I was in a light, friendly room with large windows through which I saw the blue sky and white cumulus clouds. I was alone and noticed that I had a tube in my mouth. I was propped upright on pillows in bed. From now on I had only one wish – to get well as soon as possible to make my film about Africa. I still could not speak and did not know that the doctors considered my return to consciousness a miracle.

As soon as I could move my fingers and speak a little, I sent an optimistic telegram to my mother in Munich to tell her all was well. But my euphoria was misguided. After my broken ribs had healed quite quickly, the doctor told me that my lung had collapsed, injured by the broken ribs. My condition would make it impossible for me to be flown to Germany, and the operation on the lung would have to be performed on the spot.

In the middle of the village a group of Maasai had congregated, carrying shields and spears and wearing brass rings round their necks and chests. Their skin was not as dark as that of other Africans, more of an intense brown. Many of them had beautiful features, and they appeared cold, reserved, and were taciturn. With their arrogant expression and proud gait they moved like strangers or members of an aristocratic caste

Now, for the first time, I felt afraid. I learned that the senior consultant, Professor Cohn, and his deputy were on leave, and I refused to give permission for this serious operation. My condition deteriorated. Every day a long thick needle was stuck through my back into my lung to prevent a thrombosis. The young English doctors were very worried and tried, without success, to persuade me to have the operation. All my life I have followed my feelings rather than reason, and my feelings warned me against this operation.

When Dr. Cohn returned he examined me and found that the lung had re-inflated itself like a balloon. To the doctors I was a medical enigma. From then on my recovery progressed amazingly quickly without an operation. Less than six weeks after the accident I was able to get up and take my first steps.

16

When George Six, still walking with a stick and limping, came to visit me my joy was indescribable. He returned every day, bringing fruit and chocolate. Finally he suggested I leave the hospital secretly and proposed that he would drive me to Arusha where his wife would nurse me back to health. He proposed to collect me in his car the first time I was allowed into the garden. The flight from the hospital was easy.

When I sat next to Six in a landrover once more I forgot the accident and pain. I soaked up the African landscape with even greater fervour than during my first journey.

Suddenly I took George Six by the arm and exclaimed, 'Stop, stop!'

He looked at me in amazement and followed my glance. At the edge of the road I saw two regal figures. With long steps, without giving our car a glance, they strode ahead of us. They were dressed in ochre robes, knotted on one side. On their heads they wore strange ornaments of tall black ostrich plumes. They carried spears and shields.

Until that moment I had not seen African poeple in their traditional costumes but only dressed in European clothes. I was thrilled by the beauty of the two figures. I took their photographs and wanted to get to know them.

Six drove on. I shouted at him, 'We've got to take them along with us.'

He said drily, 'No, they stink too much. I won't give them a lift.'

I was furious. When I turned to look back at the two men, all I could see was the red dust we had raised. The figures had vanished in the haze.

'What tribe do they belong to?' I asked.

'Maasai', Six said shortly. He wasn't interested. For me this brief meeting was a turning-point.

From the very first moment Africa gave me something I have seldom found in Germany – a spontaneous warmth, a matter-of-course frankness, a natural, trusting readiness to get to know other people.

I remember, as in a waking dream, some of the occasions when I met Maasai, members of that proud, tall shepherd and warrior tribe of East Africa.

At that time, 1956, the Maasai were still regarded as the unapproachable masters of the East African savannah. They had an aura of being untouched by civilization, unspoilt, of being inaccessible in their arrogance.

I had completely recovered from my accident and was staying in the border territory between Kenya and Tanganyika (later Tanzania), in a small place called Loitokitok.

among the other local people.

I tried to photograph them. The moment they noticed my camera, they turned away. Some scowled at me and threatened me with their sticks. The girls were so shy that they ran away the moment my camera was turned on them.

This resistance irritated me a great deal. I followed various groups on their way out of town. Occasionally I managed to take a good snapshot.

Finally my patience was rewarded. I had followed three Maasai warriors who were each carrying two spears. I ran to overtake the group. I had my Leica behind my back, walked towards them, and quickly took their photograph. To my surprise they laughed and asked to look through the viewfinder of my camera. I didn't, at that time, speak a word of Maasai. What I wouldn't have given at that moment to be able to communicate with them! The young men must have felt that I was sympathetic towards them, and that I would have liked to have known everything about them. They beckoned me to follow them, and I did so without hesitation.

Soon we were outside the town. I lost all feeling of place and time. The Maasai, leaving the road, walked straight through the undergrowth and brush. The only trees in this countryside are umbrella-acacias, and with their widespread tops and the filigree of their leaves they looked unreal against the blue African sky and made the wide landscape more immense.

Sometimes the Maasai stopped, imitated animal and bird calls, showed me how they hunted wild beasts, how they stalked them, took cover, tracked them, and how they used their spears. They used sign language to try to explain all this, and I did not take any photographs because I did not want to destroy the magic of the moment. It was beautiful and exciting to watch the supple movements of the young Maasai.

After a while I became uneasy. I knew I would not be able to find my way back, for I have little sense of direction. Dusk was beginning to fall. I stood still, wanting to take my leave from them, but the Maasai shook their heads and pointed ahead. One of them formed a bowl with his hands and pretended to be drinking. Then they took me by the hand and I had to go with them. The strangeness as well as the possible danger of my position had not struck me until that moment, but now I had no choice, and my interest, my curiosity, the drug of Africa, were stronger than my fear.

We went at a pretty good pace along a narrow path, one Maasai in front, two behind me. After about half an hour we reached the kraal, the first one I had seen. An old Maasai opened a gate in the thorn hedge surrounding the kraal, and children, girls and women came to greet the returning warriors.

I was introduced to an old Maasai, obviously the chief. Then many hands were stretched out to me, and I had to shake them all. I could detect none of the arrogance I had noticed in the market place of Loitokitok. Their warriors had brought me to the kraal – and the Maasai accepted me.

A small stool was brought for me, while the rest of them squatted in a circle around me. A Maasai girl brought a calabash of fresh milk, and now I understood what the warrior had meant by his drinking gesture. Though I was secretly afraid that the milk might contain bacteria, I felt I must not offend the Maasai, and I drank and smiled, for all eyes were on me. After I had drunk the milk and thanked them, one of the Maasai who had brought me came up to me and indicated with gestures that he would take me back. I was speechless, for I had not expected this after everything I had been told about the Maasai.

It was dark when my Maasai said goodbye to me in the Loitokitok market place. He said something I did not understand, perhaps his name, perhaps a greeting. I never saw him again.

My second meeting with these strange, fascinating people was also an adventure and gave me a completely new perspective on the Maasai. I had lost my way in the Tanzanian steppe in the landrover. I was circling around helplessly, when two figures appeared on the horizon. They were two Maasai with shields and spears, their hair done curiously in small plaits. I drove towards them, stopped, and asked the way in English although this was really quite pointless.

To my surprise, one of the Maasai replied in good English. I was amazed.

'How do you come to speak English so well?' I asked him.

'I learned it at school.'

'Where did you go to school?'

'First in Nairobi, then in London.'

'What were you doing in London?'

'I took my PhD there. I am a teacher.'

I was perplexed. This man looked like the classical tribal warrior in a picture in a book on ethnology. And he had a degree in philology!

'Why are you walking around here then, in this get-up?' I asked.

He smiled and said, 'I like to be a Maasai.'

This short answer moved me deeply. It formed a bridge between tradition and the present, the primitive and civilization. I have loved the Maasai ever since, and in the years that have gone by I have been deeply conscious of the sadness of seeing these impressive and naturally proud people degraded, through the plague of civilization, into today's inhabitants of corrugated iron huts. Only few Maasai can, like this teacher who carried shield and spear, both preserve the old and come to terms with the new.

My feelings for Africa have changed, for grief for the lost paradise has long joined my original euphoria. But what Ernest Hemingway says in *Green Hills of Africa* still holds good for me:

'All I wanted to do now was get back to Africa. We had not left it, yet, but when I would wake in the night I would lie, listening, homesick for it already.'

An English official who lived for years among the Maasai told me that English colonial civil servants had long ago stopped putting Maasai in prison for stealing cattle. The desire for freedom of the Maasai is so strong that they refuse food in prison and die. Another penalty was therefore devised by which a Maasai had to hand over his favourite cow. To understand the harshness of this punishment one has to realise that cattle are the soul of the Maasai. They have an almost magic relationship with their animals. For the Maasai, his favourite cow is his most treasured possession.

When one young Maasai was sentenced to hand over his favourite cow he suffered to such an extent seeing his cow publicly branded to show that it would be someone else's property that, in his despair, he killed the English official who had convicted him. He then allowed himself to be taken away though he knew that he would have to pay for this deed with his life.

What followed is amazing. The Maasai warrior's clan condemned his action. They then sold many of their cattle and gave the money to the dead Englishman's family so that his eldest son could go to London to study.

It was in the desert north of Isiolo in northern Kenya that I met a Bedouin for the first time. There were no settlements anywhere and, what was worse, there was no water. The night was starry and cool. I put on a thick woollen sweater and sat down on the iron box which held my photographic equipment. My eye roamed over the moonlit desert landscape in its magnificent emptiness.

Suddenly, as if conjured out of the ground, a dark-skinned boy stood before me. He pointed into the distance, a gesture which invited me to follow him. He was dressed like a nomad, with a light-coloured cloth knotted at the shoulder. Lightfooted, he strode ahead. After some time we could see the silhouette of a group of palms. Not a voice nor a noise could be heard, only the sound of our footsteps. It was as if time had stood still. Then we reached the palms. Out of their shadow stepped a large man. He came to meet us and invited us with a gesture to follow him. We entered a nomad camp fenced by closely woven straw mats. Inside the camp lay and stood camels, donkeys, goats and other animals. The nomad offered us a bowl of strong-tasting camels milk.

The starry sky, the palms, the camels, the Bedouin – it was like a picture from the bible. After a time our eyes became accustomed to the darkness and we saw a few tents made of straw mats. Our host allowed us to look into one of them. On a wide, neatly woven mat lay a beautiful young woman with long, pitch-black hair. She was not veiled but was swathed in colourful embroidered fabrics. She wore many gold bangles. She did not seem embarrassed.

After she had exchanged a few words with her husband, he took us to the second tent. Here too a woman, wearing many gold ornaments, slightly older but still beautiful, lay on a straw carpet. Full of pride he showed us the third tent, where a very young woman lay, a small child in her arms.

Our host must have been a very wealthy Bedouin to have had three tents and three wives. I found this glance into a strange world bewildering. It seems to me inconceivable that these people will one day have to give up their freedom because our world has no room for this kind of existence.

We were given dates and figs and then said goodbye. All this was done with gestures – life can be very simple.

Yes, life was very simple in that Africa which has now vanished and yet remains so close to me. I can still see it when I think of it in the daytime, and I often see it in my dreams. I saw paradise, and I want to tell everybody about it – for it has vanished like a mirage.

It was in 1962 that I first went with an expedition to look for the Nubians of Kordofan. Let me tell it in the present tense, since for me it is happening at this very moment.

We have been travelling for some hours. The roads are very bad, and we have to drive carefully. Now and again we meet men and women who give us a friendly greeting. They are probably Nubians, but how are we to recognise them? They are wearing European clothes, even sun glasses, and there is no indication what tribe they belong to. We occasionally come across Baggara nomads, their entire goods and gear loaded on cattle, who move past us on their migration. We meet fewer and fewer people, the countryside becomes more and more empty. We feel a little depressed, and though none of us will actually say so, we all feel that the extraordinary phenomenon we are looking for will be hard to find.

I remember what the chief of police of El Obeid had told me,

'You are ten years too late.' This thought makes me suddenly feel very tired. I wipe the dust from my face and drink several mugs of water in quick succession from the waterbag which always hangs on the outside of our vehicle. We drive on.

Our cars brush through high grass. Large rocks and ancient trees make the country look like a mythical landscape. One might well see Pan here, sitting on a rock playing his pipe. The mountains seem to close in on us. The valley becomes narrower. Several times we have to drive through deep ditches and dry riverbeds, first moving some rocks out of the way. I keep being surprised how well the trucks manage this terrain. No animals. No water anywhere. I look at my watch, we've been travelling for nine hours. The sun will be setting in two hours. The road becomes more and more stony.

Suddenly we notice round huts on the mountain slopes, stuck against the rocks like birdsnests. Nubian houses! My tiredness has vanished. We drive closer to the slopes and stop. A long-legged young girl stands on a rock swinging a switch. She is naked. Only a string of red beads decorates her black body. Startled she looks at us, then leaps away like a gazelle and vanishes in the bush.

We drive on, full of hope and curiosity, but once more we see no people or animals. We are surrounded by a great silence. The sun is already beginning to turn red. We can only drive at walking pace now since large roots and stones are in the way. At last we have to stop for the terrain has become impassable.

We are just about to turn back when we see a group of strangely adorned people in the distance. We decide to follow them cautiously on foot. We notice that they are led by a group of tall men whose bodies have been whitened with ash. They are naked and wear strange ornaments on their heads. They are followed by other tall men whose athletic bodies are painted with decorations. Girls and women walk at the end of the group, also painted and adorned with bead ornaments. They carry calabashes and large baskets on their heads and walk beautifully erect and light-footed behind the group of men. At last we have found the Nubians.

The path mounts pretty steeply over scree and sloping slabs of rock. Then the Nubian group suddenly vanishes. A large rock obstructs our view. When we have walked around it, we stand amazed, before us a spectacle so overwhelming, so strange, that it is difficult to describe.

One or two thousand people are swaying in the light of the setting sun in an open space surrounded by many trees. Strangely painted, fantastically adorned, they appear like creatures from another planet. Hundreds of spear-points dance

22

against the background of the glowing red sun. In the middle of this multitude, large and small circles have formed in which pairs of pugilists challenge each other, fight, dance, and are borne as victors out of the ring on the shoulders of their friends.

I am dazed and don't know what to photograph first. Everything I see is strange, extraordinary and tremendously fascinating. It is not only what we see which creates this exotic atmosphere, the strange sounds we hear contribute to it. A ceaseless drumming and above it the high trilling of women's voices, added to the cries of the crowd all create an exciting tension. I have long lost my companions and find myself in the middle of the crowd. Hands are stretched out to me, faces smile at me, I feel that I am with good people.

The pugilist bouts seem to be at an end, for I see more and more groups of ash-painted, white pugilists coming towards me, dancing. They stamp their feet which have bells attached to them, bend their heavy trunks far forwards, and dance, their hands held bent back, as gracefully as Balinese temple dancers. At the same time they utter deep cries which remind me of animal voices. I can hardly tear myself away from the sight of these figures which appear even more mysterious in the twilight.

After this incredible experience I lost all feeling of the passage of time. I know from the notes in my diary that this first Nubian pugilist festival took place on December 16th 1962, and that we found a place to camp on December 22nd where we planned to remain for the time being. This was an ideal spot with the necessary shade for our vehicles under a tree whose branches projected almost thirty metres. It was close to the Nubian settlement, and, what was most important, only three kilometres from a well.

Sleeping under this tree the first night, I could not believe that I was really there.

The Nubians gave me unforgettable pictorial memories which unroll like a long film. I will conjure up these pictures just as they rise to the surface, without chronological order, without ethnological explanation. They are pictures which might have come out of mythology, pictures, I believe, of everlasting magic. A personal letter of 1962 will perhaps show how deep this feeling of Africa was and is. This is a letter to my beloved mother, written on Christmas day 1962 in the Nubian mountains.
'Dearest Mother,

'I don't know when or whether you will receive this letter, for we are deep in the heart of the Sudan and will only be able to post our letters when we get to Kadugli. Yesterday, on Chrismas eve, my thoughts were with you.
'You cannot imagine how simply we live here, but you

can believe me when I tell you that this life, unburdened of all the appurtenances of our civilization, is somehow very liberating. What I find particularly marvellous is the fact that we spend all day and night in the fresh air, that we aren't disturbed by newspapers or the telephone, and lose no time over our wardrobe. But that isn't all. The Nubians among whom we are living here are so cheerful that I am never bored. They trust us more and more. You should have seen us last night. We were sitting on our wooden boxes eating our evening meal, but we couldn't move an inch. The Nubians had sat down on all the boxes beside us, especially the girls and boys. About a hundred Nubians had gathered in a circle around us, so close that they were barely a yard from us. The reason they came so near was no doubt our radio on which we were trying to receive the German Africa transmission which is broadcast from Cologne and transmitted by way of Khartoum. It was strange to hear the Christmas carols so deep in Africa. The Nubians too listened with great interest. It must have been very strange for them, but they seemed to enjoy it very much. In the background I could see men with spears, but in the front there were mainly old people, women and adolescents, and the tiny children who sat on the ground right in front of us.

'Because of the Christmas festivities there was a little glass of brandy. It was a wonderful and strange Christmas eve, I am only sorry that for once I had to spend it without you, dearest mother. But my thoughts are with you. Please don't worry about me, I am happy and well and I shall write to you as often as possible.

'Yours, Leni.'

When I met the Nubians they were in a state of innocence. They did not know about money, they lived by barter and therefore neither envied nor claimed other people's possessions. They respected each other, and in today's phraseology one would say that they lived in ecological harmony with each other and the world around them. It is money and the influences of civilization – from films to prostitution – that have banished them in an alarmingly short time, from their inner paradise. By 1967-1968 the pollution of their world had advanced so far that it broke my heart.

It will perhaps be said that I idealised the Nubians of that time too much, projecting on to them my own desire for an ideal world. But there are other witnesses, such as my companion Horst who came with me three times to visit the Nubians. He and others will confirm that in those years the world of the Nubians was still a good world.

The Mesakin Nubians in particular – for I wouldn't like to lump together all the Nubians, let alone all primitive peoples – were in those days people whose qualities moved me deeply. They were childlike, peace loving, not at all proud, they were attached to their families and blessed with a happy balanced social structure. There was no crime, the land was owned communally, and the old and sick were looked after by the community as a matter of course. Their religious rituals seemed to me to have remained unspoilt, the world of their beliefs remained untouched. This was demonstrated by their pugilist festivals. I will try and describe their magical qualities.

We could hear the sound of drums in one of the huts. In the darkness of the room we could at first make out no more than one light-coloured figure. A young Nubian sat on the floor, immobile and quite lost in thought. He had been covered with ash from head to foot, and looked not so much like a man of flesh and blood as like a marble sculpture.

A few young Nubian men who had not been covered in ash stood near him and watched him with strangely serious expressions. Some women too were unable to take their eyes off the young man. The drumming came from a dark corner. There was a feeling of solemnity in the dark room, and I guessed that by a stroke of luck I was witnessing the consecration of a young man.

Very carefully, so as not to disturb anyone, I took a few photographs. Nobody took any notice. Then a young man approached the youth and scattered ash over him. The youth remained completely immobile. He seemed to be meditating.

A tall older man then stepped into the middle of the room. Over his arm he carried many lengths of coloured materials as well as white fur-ornaments decorated with shells. He held the young man's garments as if they were precious objects. He appeared to be the youth's father. The boy got up, the same inturned look still on his face, and while he slowly lifted his arms, the young men wound the bands of material around his body. Everyone gazed at the youth with rapture while he was being adorned more and more magnificently. Nothing now recalled the Nubian youth he had formerly been – he looked exotic, like a puppet in a Chinese play.

A beam of sunshine came through the roof of the hut and fell on the young man in his splendid apparel. I had never had the opportunity to take so unique a photograph.

After the robing ceremony, ash was once more thrown over the youth, so that his clothes were covered. A loud drumroll, and the youth threw up his arms as if awaking from his numbness, uttered muffled sounds and began to make dance movements

25

with his hands. His fingers moved as rapidly as the wings of a dragonfly. Suddenly the youth bent down, taking up the initial stance of a pugilist. A powerful, naked Nubian stood opposite him.

Now followed a fascinating spectacle. The two men performed a dance imitating a pugilist bout. Lithe as two large cats – one black and one white – they mimed each phase of a fight. They dodged, they attacked and whirled through the room in the shimmering ash-dust, until the youth had won a symbolic victory. This ceremony made him a *kaduma* and enabled him to compete with the most powerful pugilists for the first time.

Then all the Nubians, led by the youth, left the hut to the sound of drumrolls and the blowing of horns. At five o'clock we reached the ground where the festival was held. The bouts were already in full swing. Hundreds of Nubians had assembled amongst the large rocks and old trees.

Tukami, a young man from 'our' village stood crouched in the typical pugilistic stance before a truly gigantic Nubian who was trying to touch Tukami's head with his long arms. But Tukami evaded him cleverly, moving at lightning speed. Then he went back to the same position, elbows on thighs, shoulders moving casually, but his eyes never leaving his opponent, fixed in total concentration.

When they began to wrestle the crowd became more and more excited, the circle moved closer and closer. The Nubian giant tried to catch Tukami by the leg, but he, lithe as a panther, evaded him in a way that was a mystery to me. Then each tried to turn his opponent's body by sheer exertion, shoulder to shoulder. The loser was the one who first touched the ground with any part of his back. A referee watched each bout and separated the pugilists if the bout went on too long without a decision.

When I had both of them splendidly in my viewfinder they suddenly moved directly towards me . . . and fell right over me. I was buried under them with my Leica and wrenched my shoulder which was very painful. The contenders quickly helped me up, and, instead of being angry and chasing me away, they laughed and felt my limbs to see if anything was broken. We only found out next day that I had broken several ribs, and I had to be taken to the hospital in Kadugli where an adhesive bandage was put on so that I was able to return to my Nubians at once.

Another picture, another festival. There was a full moon and the African landscape lay in its magical light. More and more Nubians began to walk about the bright moonlight in groups and in pairs. All the young people had come to flirt and have fun. I noticed that the couples holding hands were either young men or girls. I never saw Nubian men and girls walk hand in hand.

The later it got the more lively and high-spirited the occasion became. There were endless gusts of laughter, girls shrieking as they were chased by the men, the air full of laughter and song. Then I heard the drums.

I noticed how the girls and men put their arms about each other's waists, formed a small circle and moved first to one side then to the other with short dance steps, stamping their feet. The girls wore small bells around their ankles, and with these they emphasized the fast rhythm of the dance. As they stamped their feet they shot out their chins, singing their songs. The Nubians call these dances *oku*, and they were danced on moonlit nights. In the middle of the circle a young Nubian stood or sat, leading the songs like a sort of choirmaster. The words of the songs were improvisations on the events of the day.

Most of the Nubian girls were very pretty and had enchanting figures, tall slim legs, very narrow hips, beautifully formed arms and hands, broad but finely made shoulders, and a long, slim neck. The most noticeable feature of the unmarried girls was their beautifully shaped breasts.

This *oku* festival is often the occasion for men to choose their brides, but an outsider would not notice this. The young men approached the girls very unobtrusively, almost shyly. Eyes and hands were used to woo the opposite sex. A Nubian girl who showed her feelings too plainly would have no chance with a Nubian man, however pretty she was. This led to the Nubian girls wearing a proud and self-confident expression. Even when a girl was very much in love, she would make a show of rebuffing the man who would have to continue to woo her. Such a courtship could last for weeks, even months. Only when the girl was convinced that he preferred her to all others would she drop all pretence and show her liking by laughing and flirting with the man of her choice. But even then the man had to be patient, waiting for the girl to show that she was ready by snapping her fingers three times. Then they would disappear into the country-side one night. Such scenes remain for ever in my memory.

The south-eastern Nubians, whom I called the 'People of Kau' in my book of photographs, were quite different. I called them this because Kau, the largest of their three villages was where we had our camp. Apart from Kau there was Nyaro and Fungor. The number of south-eastern Nubians is estimated to be only three thousand. When I visited the tribe for the first time in 1974 I was stunned. I had never seen anything like it. Though I was only able to stay three days on my first visit, I was able to take some unique photographs. These Nubians had been even less touched by civilization than the Mesakin-Quisar Nubians. Now the photographs have made them world-famous. But signs of decline could already be seen in 1974 when I went there for the first time with my collaborator Horst to record this African culture in film and photograph.

The tourist agencies who have brought foreigners to this area are to blame for the destruction of the unspoilt nature of these people. The money the tourists gave the Nubians to see a dance or a fight was the beginning of their decline. When tourist cars arrived, Horst and I hid in the Nubian houses. Our relationship with them was quite different from that of the tourists. We were friends, had never given them money, though this has often been claimed by those who have envied us. We knew that money would damage them, but instead we spent an hour or two doing medical work every day when dusk fell. Many a time Horst had to see to gaping wounds. There was a geat deal of work for us, especially after the knife-fights. We did it gladly and were able to help many of the Nubians.

After many weeks of heavy work in the fields around the villages, the Nubians came home, and a time of festivals and the painting of masks began. There is probably no other tribe in the whole world that spends as much time and artistic skill on this as the south-eastern Nubians. The inspired way they paint their bodies and faces would have delighted Picasso. Where did they get this gift? Nobody knows. The girls are unusually beautiful, and this beauty is enhanced by the way they paint themselves from top to toe with a mixture of oil and colours. To see them go about among the rocks and huts, painted red, yellow, brown and black, is utterly unreal, fantastic, exotic. They wear no clothes apart from their bead ornaments and a belt. The girls and men of the south-eastern Nubians do not go about without a belt, though they wear no other clothes, for they feel naked without it. And it is only when they are young and healthy that they wear no clothes. A young Nubian who is ill will wear a gallibiya, an Arab robe, even if his illness is a minor one. When a girl becomes pregnant, she always wears a long piece of material swinging from her hips. The Nubians' sense of beauty is so strongly developed that they have different names for every posture of the body.

They come to me in my dreams, not as human beings, but as strange impalpable creatures fashioned by artists. That is how they will live in my memory, and not as they are now, wearing sun glasses, ugly clothes and clumsy shoes. At the very last moment, before everything changed, I was able to capture the Nubians as they once were.

I was staying in Malakal on the White Nile in the region of the Shilluk when I was able to persuade a German Africa-traveller to make a trip into the Nubian mountains. This was a risky enterprise, since this region is full of swampy terrain. There were weeks to go before the steppe would have dried out. Some hundreds of kilometres lay before us. We had maps, but since there were no roads in this region, merely tracks which were only passable in the dry season, it was impossible to know whether we would be able to drive on the connecting stretches. The German demanded 1,500 Marks in advance for the trip which was calculated to last a month, including a stay with the Nubians. But since I had only 1,880 Marks and had to travel to Nairobi afterwards, it was a great deal of money to lay out.

We had meant to start in the morning, but had to buy provisions. There were many bazaars in Malakal where one could buy tinned food. We waited beside the Nile for the last ferry to take us to the other bank. Already the sun was low in the sky, and I watched Shilluk fishermen on the quietly flowing river as, with their long spears, they skillfully caught large fish. Their long, narrow boats rocked alarmingly, and my heart was in my mouth, as I thought of the many crocodiles which lie in wait for their prey at this time of the evening.

As we crossed the Nile on the ferry, the sun sank below the horizon of the endless steppe which lay before us. The three of us sat in the front of the VW bus which was packed to the roof behind us. I sat between the German who was driving and an Englishman of whom I knew no more than that he was always drawing.

To our left and right the lonely, treeless steppe went by, no huts, no human being in sight. The German drove well; now and again he was able to follow the track of other vehicles. He wanted to go as far as Tonga, about 80 kilometres from the Nile. Tonga is a small Shilluk village which has an American mission station. We hoped to spend the night there. But things turned out differently.

When we stopped, I thought at first that the engine had stalled. But when the German and the Englishman got out, and I heard the German swearing, I feared the worst. I left the car and immediately noticed that it was marshy underfoot. A glance at the wheels was enough to convince me that we had met with a catastrophe. All four wheels of the car were stuck in the swamp. Getting out was quite out of the question. I was appalled and imagined that this was the end of my trip to the Nubians.

Nobody said a word. The silence was eerie. There was no hope of a passing vehicle. We couldn't stay there. Help had to be fetched, and help could only come from Malakal. I didn't know how far we had come, but since it was still dusk I guessed the distance from the Nile to be ten or fifteen kilometres.

I cautiously offered to walk back to the Nile to get help from Malakal if one of the men came with me. But they both refused. They wanted to stay with the car. I could't imagine how they expected to pull the car from the marsh without help when it had already sunk up to its axle in the mud.

What was I to do? To stay and hope for a miracle was madness. I decided to go by myself.

I ran as fast I could to get as far as possible before nightfall. The sky was red in the direction of Malakal, probable because of a steppe fire. As it got dark my pace slowed more and more, for I could see very little. I remembered that I had forgotten to bring my torch; I had left the car in far too much of a hurry but could not now turn back since I would not have been able to find it in the darkness. The way to Malakal was at least signposted by the red sky.

Slowly my eyes became used to the dark, and I went on. Suddenly I heard animal noises. I stood still and listened. I became afraid. I remembered that the German had told us that there were many kinds of animals around here, even lions since there was enough water and the lions like to take cattle from the Shilluks' herds. For a long time I did not dare to move.

When finally I could hear nothing but the light wind, I continued carefully. After I had walked for a little more than an hour, I saw two dim points of light in the distance. At first I thought they were the eyes of an animal, a wild beast. The lights became larger as I got closer. I strained to see what it was. Then I saw the silhouette of a man approaching me. A Shilluk stood before me and, to my surprise, addressed me in good English. He was startled to meet me here alone. He had ridden his tricycle from the bank of the Nile and told me that he worked at the American mission in Tonga to which he was returning.

I told him of our accident, and he said I could not possibly continue on my own and offered to drive me as far as the Nile. I accepted his help gratefully. I sat in front of him on his tricycle, and we rode towards the river. When we got to the bank, he asked me to wait. He wanted to go in search of a Shilluk who could take me to Malakal in a boat. I sat down on a rock and waited for what seemed at the time an eternity before my rescuer returned. I had been bitten all over by mosquitoes.

He had found a Shilluk who was willing to row me to Malakal in his boat. When I had thanked the Shilluk from the mission and said goodbye to him, he presented me with his bead bracelet.

I was now quite alone with the strange Shilluk. The night was beautiful as a dream, the air full of low chirping and humming, like faint music. The immense starry sky was stretched above the dark landscape like a huge tent. The stars appeared close and large and shimmered and glittered more brightly than I had ever seen before. We glided across the Nile without a sound. I thought of the many crocodiles, but the Shilluk steered the small boat, a hollowed-out tree-trunk, with so much skill, that my fear dwindled.

When we reached Malakal the lights still burned in the town. When I had paid the Shilluk and made as if to say good-bye to him he gave me to understand that he wanted to continue to accompany me. We walked along the bank of the Nile, then took a wide road leading to the town. He took me to the police station and spoke a few words in Arabic to the Sudanese policemen. I once more pressed his hand in gratitude, then he vanished into the darkness.

The three policemen looked at me with curiosity. After all it was not every day that a white woman, alone but for a Shilluk, arrived at the police station in Malakal. Unfortunately none of the Sudanese spoke English, and I did not speak Arabic. I was offered a chair, and someone brought me a lemonade while one of the policemen unsuccessfully cranked the handle of the telephone. I was beginning to feel more and more hungry, but was too embarrassed to ask the policemen for something to eat. Then one of the policemen got through on the telephone, and I was made to understand that someone was coming for me.

With hunger came tiredness. I could have lain down on the floor and gone to sleep. Still fighting sleep, I heard the sound of a car. It was the adjutant of the governor of the province of the Upper Nile. When I told him everything that had happened, he said, 'No problem. We'll get the car out of the marsh for you tomorow.' Then he took me to a small hotel near the airport.

Without anything to eat, exhausted but happy, I slept in a bed with clean sheets for the first time in three months.

Punctually at seven o'clock in the morning my escort came to collect me. I was amazed to see three large military trucks with a dozen soldiers in front of the hotel. The first ferry of the day took us across the Nile. In no time at all we had found the car which, of course, was still stuck in the mud. The German and the Englishman were sitting under a mosquito net having breakfast. The soldiers got down to work immediately. Using tow-ropes, they extricated the car within a few minutes and put it back on solid ground. Now we would be able to continue our journey into the promised land of the Nubians . . .

Another adventure remains vividly in my mind. From Malakal I wanted to visit the country of the Dinkas. An Arab gave me a lift in a military vehicle. For hours we drove over a bumpy track. Suddenly we saw three Dinkas. Until then I had had hardly any opportunities for taking photographs of Dinkas, and the ones we saw at that moment seemed absolutely ideal with their traditional wide bead belts and their spears.

When I asked the Arab to stop he did not want to do so. He was afraid. At that time the troubles in the south had just started. But I managed to persuade him and got out. The Dinkas stood there quite peacefully. I showed them my Leica. One of the Dinkas explained by sign language that they wanted money to be photographed. I nodded, for they fascinated me. I had quite forgotten that I had no money with me.

I quickly took some photographs, then went back to the car. The Dinkas followed me. I put my hand out to take some money from my old handbag. At that moment I felt hot and cold all over – I didn't have a single coin with me. I searched and searched. The Dinkas came closer, threateningly it seemed to me.

Suddenly there weren't just three Dinkas but ten. The sweat stood out on the Arab's forehead.

More and more Dinkas appeared. I had no idea where they all came from. We were almost surrounded. In my panic I grabbed an old brass tobacco tin someone had given me in Malakal. Instinctively I held up the glittering object. The Dinkas stared spellbound at the tobacco tin. Then I raised my arm and hurled it as far as I could into the grass. The Dinkas flung themselves on the box.

The Arab quickly turned on the ignition. The car started and began to move forward across the muddy ground, but slowly and with alarming jerks. The disappointed Dinkas ran after us, threatening us, their spears pointing at the car. If the car had got stuck in the mud, we would have had no chance of surviving. This was the only time during my many journeys through Africa that I found myself in a dangerous situation. But it was, of course, my own fault, and no doubt such incidents were necessary to experience Africa to the full.

I now want to come back to the dramatic events following my car accident in northern Kenya. I was at that time looking for ideas for my film *Black Cargo*. After a delay of two months I was able to start the preliminary work at Lamu, a peninsula on the coast of Kenya.

Every year at the time of the monsoon, hundreds of large and small sailing boats used to arrive from India, first calling at the island of Zanzibar. They mostly brought cloth and silver ornaments from India and took back other goods, chiefly valuable wood. Among these sailing ships, the dhows, there were also some that traded in slaves. When they left Zanzibar, mostly in February or March, many of them stopped at Lamu before their voyage home. Here they anchored for some time to load the red cedar wood which had been piled up on the waterfront. But in lonely bays on dark nights, men who had been abducted from their homes were also bundled into the boats while the wood was being loaded. On the return journey they were sold as slaves in southern Arabian countries.

The chief of police at Lamu told me of the difficulties in prosecuting the slave traders. They operated with such cunning, that the English police had never yet been able to catch them. Though the police had the use of fast motorboats with which they could catch up with the sailing boats and stop them, this did not help. The slave traders took simple but infallible precautionary measures. The moment a motor boat stopped a sailing boat in which there were slaves, a hatch in the sailing boat was opened. The men destined for slavery were hidden, chained hand and foot, under the cargo of wood in the bowels of the ship. Each had a heavy stone tied to the fetters on his feet. If the police checked a boat they were invariably unable to find the unfortunate men, for the crew had long since pushed them into the sea through the hatch.

It would take us too far afield if I were to go more deeply into the slave trade and its victims, but I want to relate how my projected film came to founder. For one thing we had lost two months through my accident. Since the film could only be shot in the dry season, the time lost could not be made up. Then came the Suez war. This meant that our film equipment, cameras, lights and other things, arrived in Mombasa in Kenya weeks late, since the boats had to go all the way round Africa. We were in despair. Then there appeared another, quite unexpected problem.

In the film *Black Cargo*, the casting of the parts of the slaves was particularly important. They had to be played by big, muscular men, for the stronger the slaves were, the higher the price the slave traders received for them. When I was writing the script I did not know that there were no such athletic men in East Africa. I had imagined that it would be quite easy to cast these parts.

The reality was quite different. The tribes who live in East Africa, the Maasai, Samburu, Turkana, etc., are mostly slender, even gaunt. The slave traders collected their 'wares' from the Congo, the Sudan, and from Central Africa. Since I did not want to give up the idea of the film under any circumstances, as it was the first chance I had had since the war to make a film, I was undaunted by any difficulties. I had to find actors who would fit the parts of the slaves. I had noticed that some of the policemen were of the size and had the massive bodies I was looking for. What followed was one of my most exciting adventures in Africa.

In Mombasa I waited, nervous and impatient, four days for the party. Anxiously I met every train from Nairobi. At last, on the fifth day, I saw my Arab get off the train. He looked sad and tired, and I had a premonition that all was not well. What had happened? He told me that all twelve men had appeared at the station the following day, but that, when the train had arrived, three had run away. From then on they had disappeared one after another at every station. They had become afraid that my young Arab student was himself a slave trader. Only three of the men had come with him all the way.

I was determined to find my actors that very day, and to travel to Lamu where Mr. Six and my film crew were waiting for me. I went to the harbour in Mombasa, where I watched the stevedores carrying heavy sacks and boxes to the boats. With the help of an interpreter I spoke to them, promised them good wages, and, within a few hours, I had managed to persuade five men to come with us to Lamu the same day. I agreed to their only condition — that they should be allowed to say goodbye to their families. I bundled them into a taxi and took them from one family to the next. I could fill a whole chapter with the scenes I saw. It would make you laugh and cry.

By late afternoon we were crowded tightly in my VW bus. Time had been so short, we had not even bought provisions. At that time, in 1956, there was as yet no road between Mombasa and Lamu. The road only went as far as Malindi, and from there one had to drive on a narrow track through thick jungle.

I shall never forget that nightmare drive through the night, alone with nine unknown Africans and my Arab. It was a nightmare. From Malindi we drove in complete darkness. from the same region, a small village near Lake Victoria, not far from the Uganda border. I decided to charter a small sports plane to fly there and bring back my actors to play the slaves. Since I needed an interpreter, I engaged an Arab student who spoke both Kiswahili and English. After some adventures we reached the village near Kisuma. Everything was quickly arranged with the headman, and we received his authorization. All the men in the village were called together. Most of them were suitable for the parts, though not quite as I had imagined. Twelve men were chosen, a contract was agreed with the headman, covering pay, provisions and the period of employment, and a part-payment agreed. I was delighted to have found my actors. I was to fly back to Mombasa, and the young Arab was to follow by train with the twelve actors the next day.
Occasionally we saw the eyes of animals shining in the dark. Elephants and rhinos trotted ahead of us on the track, and we had

to drive at walking pace. Sometimes we stopped and reversed, so that the animals could get past us.

The driver suddenly stopped the bus with a jerk. Before us, in the light of the headlamps, lay a huge python, looking almost white, several metres long, and as thick as a tree-trunk. Fascinated, my heart beating violently, I watched as the snake slowly moved forwards. It seemed to take forever before it vanished into the undergrowth. In the meantime the passengers were beginning to grow restive. They became afraid that I was going to abduct them, and they also grew hungry. I had unfortunately forgotten to buy food before our nine-hour drive from Mombasa. With eleven people, our VW bus was very overloaded. The track was in appalling condition. Something like a revolt seemed about to break out among my companions. They were waving their arms and all shouting at once. I could not understand a word but was conscious that the situation was becoming critical. Just as I had remembered the gleaming tobacco tin at the moment of greatest danger from the Dinkas, so I now had a bright idea. I turned to my passengers, gestured them to be quiet, and said in Kiswahili, 'Sing'. My Arab began to sing, and one after the other they joined in. Singing, they forgot their fear and hunger. They sang until two in the morning when we reached the ocean-inlet which divided us from the Lamu Peninsula.

We woke up the boatman who was to take us to the place where we were to camp. In the boat the men were once more overcome by fear. Some of them knew that their brothers and friends had, at the end of a journey into the unknown, been taken across water to ships in which they had been taken to distant countries. I could understand their fear only too well. There was no reason why they should not take me for a slave trader. I tried to calm them with a few words of Kiswahili. At last, at four in the morning, we reached our camp which had been put up under some palms. Now my actors would be well looked after. They were soon asleep, wrapped in their woollen blankets, quite content. I too fell into a deep sleep.

Despite our hard-earned success, we soon found ourselves once more in difficulties, since the ship with our equipment did not arrive in Mombasa for five weeks. We used the time to build a special boat in Lamu for the film, and to teach our 'slaves' to row. This was quite a difficult thing to do, since they were all afraid of water. None of them was able to swim. I had to be with them in the boat all the time, to relieve them a little of their fear. When our film equipment finally arrived, dark rainclouds gathered in the sky. Once the rainy season set in it would be impossible to consider driving even as far as Mombasa, for only a few hours of rain transformed every unmade-up track into impassable mud. The leader of our expedition, Mr. Six, suggested that we should drive west as soon as possible and as far as we could, to get out of the way of the rain clouds.

Our column of cars drove almost 3,000 kilometres west just below the equator in the following two weeks, until we put up our tents on the banks of Lake Victoria near the border with Uganda. We began to film immediately and succeeded in capturing some beautiful pictures.

But after only a short time a new problem appeared. We had run out of money. The long delays had emptied our coffers. I decided to fly to Germany with the 3,000 metres of film we had shot, to raise the money necessary for the completion of the film. I needed about 80,000 Marks. Though everybody who saw the film was enthusiastic, all my efforts were unsuccessful. Then came the final blow. I received a telegram from my colleagues to tell me that after my departure all my actors had run away, my production manager had sold the equipment that was left, and the safari company had driven their boys and their landrovers back to Nairobi. That was the sad end of work on this film.

During those hours of deep discouragement I had a strange experience. I saw a photograph in the illustrated paper *Stern* which attracted me as if by magic. It showed a black athlete being carried on another's shoulders. The expression on their faces was so powerful that I cut the picture out and looked at it again and again. These two figures were exactly as I had imagined my 'black slaves', though I had never found actors to fit them. The caption under the photograph read, 'The Nubians of Kordofan'. The photograph was by the famous English photographer George Rodger.

This photograph began to influence my life like an invisible magnet. I learned that Kordofan was a province of the Sudan. Then I began to read all the books I could find about the Sudan. But I searched in vain for information about the Nubians. It was six years before I finally found 'my' Nubians and was able to live among them. That was a time of infinite happiness.

Again and again Africa has given me a tremendous feeling of freedom. That is still so today. It is the great gift Africa has given me. My Africa! It will remain with me as long as I live.

LENI RIEFENSTAHL

MAASAI

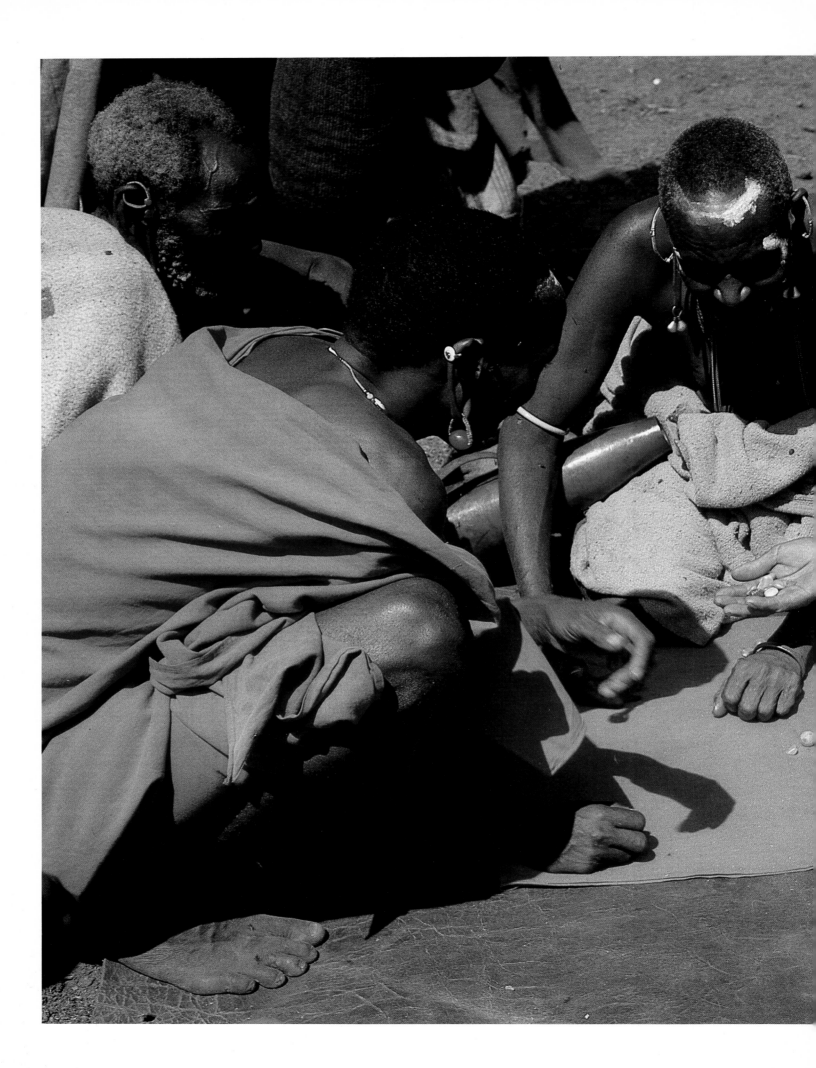

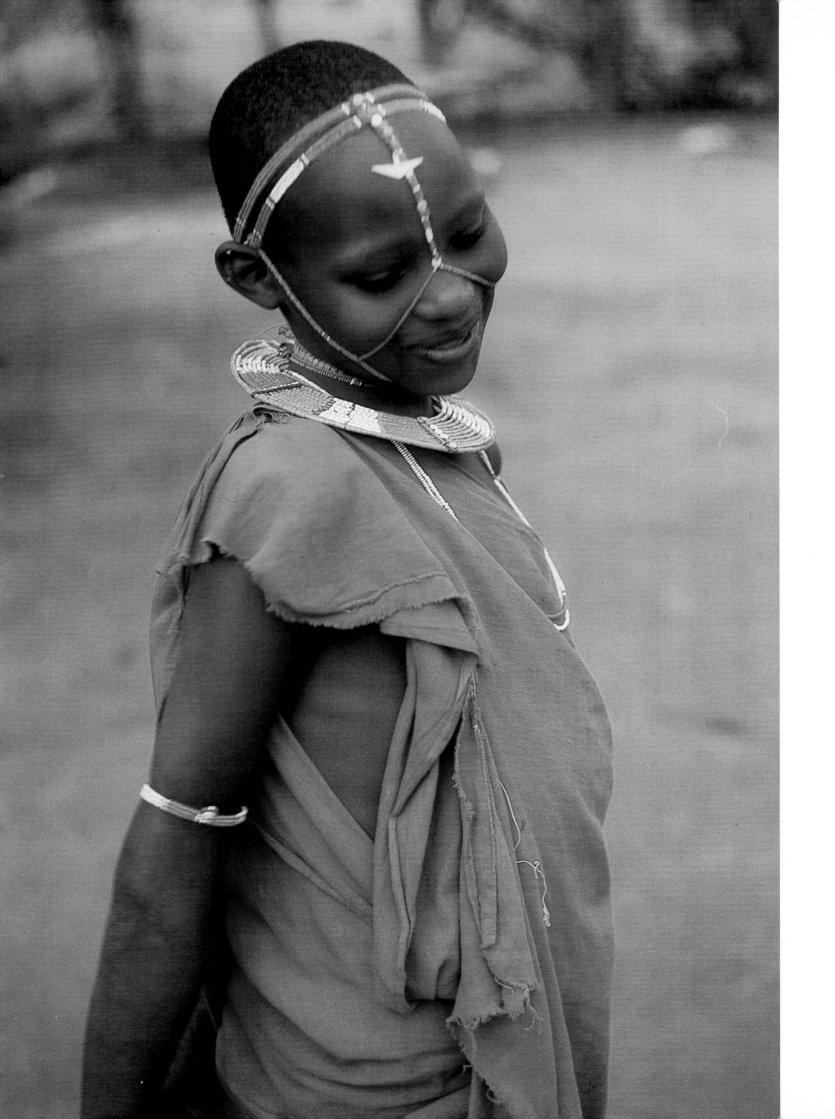

ANIMALS
IN MAASAI TERRITORY

SAMBURU

Northern Kenya

FALATA NOMADS

Southern Sudan

DINKA · MURLE ·
NUER

Southern Sudan

THE SHILLUK

Southern Sudan

THE NUBIANS ·
MESAKIN

Province of Kordofan ·
Sudan

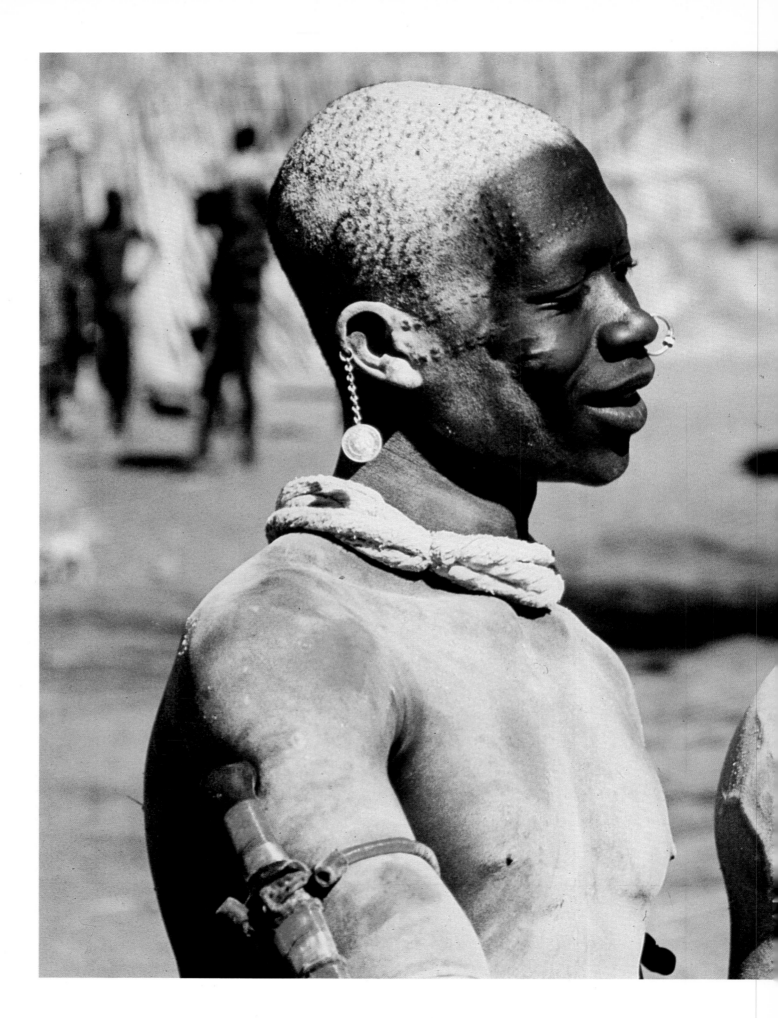

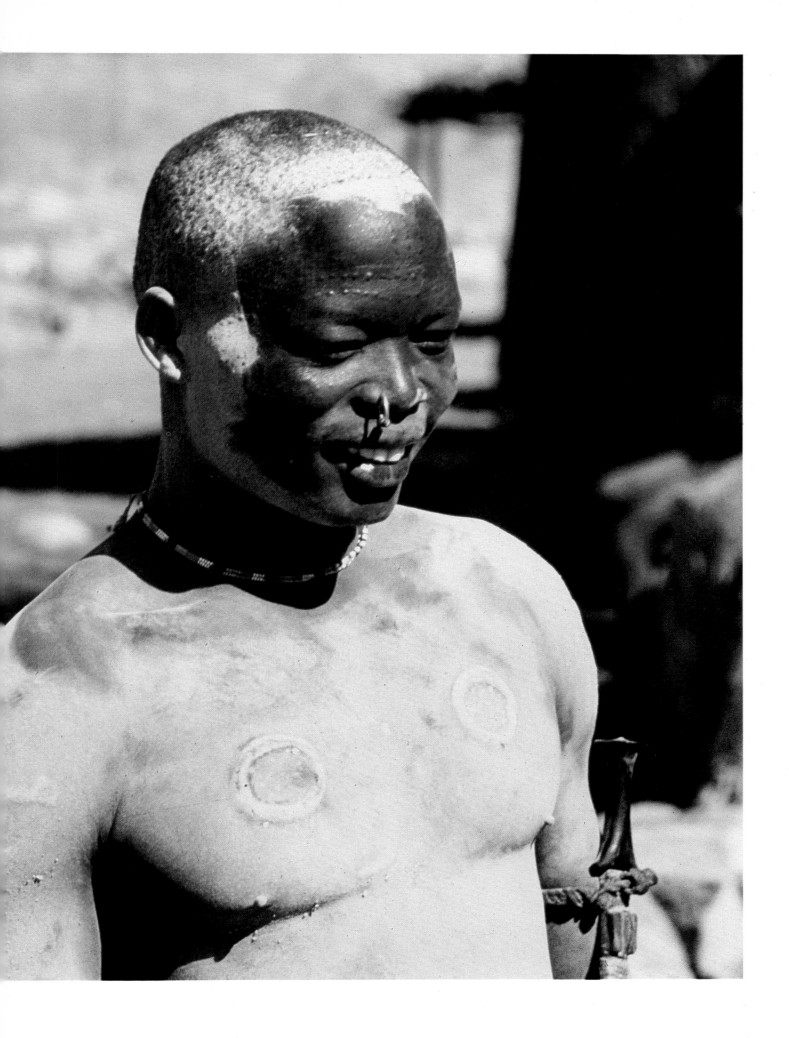

THE SOUTH-EASTERN NUBIANS

Nyaro ·Kau · Fungor

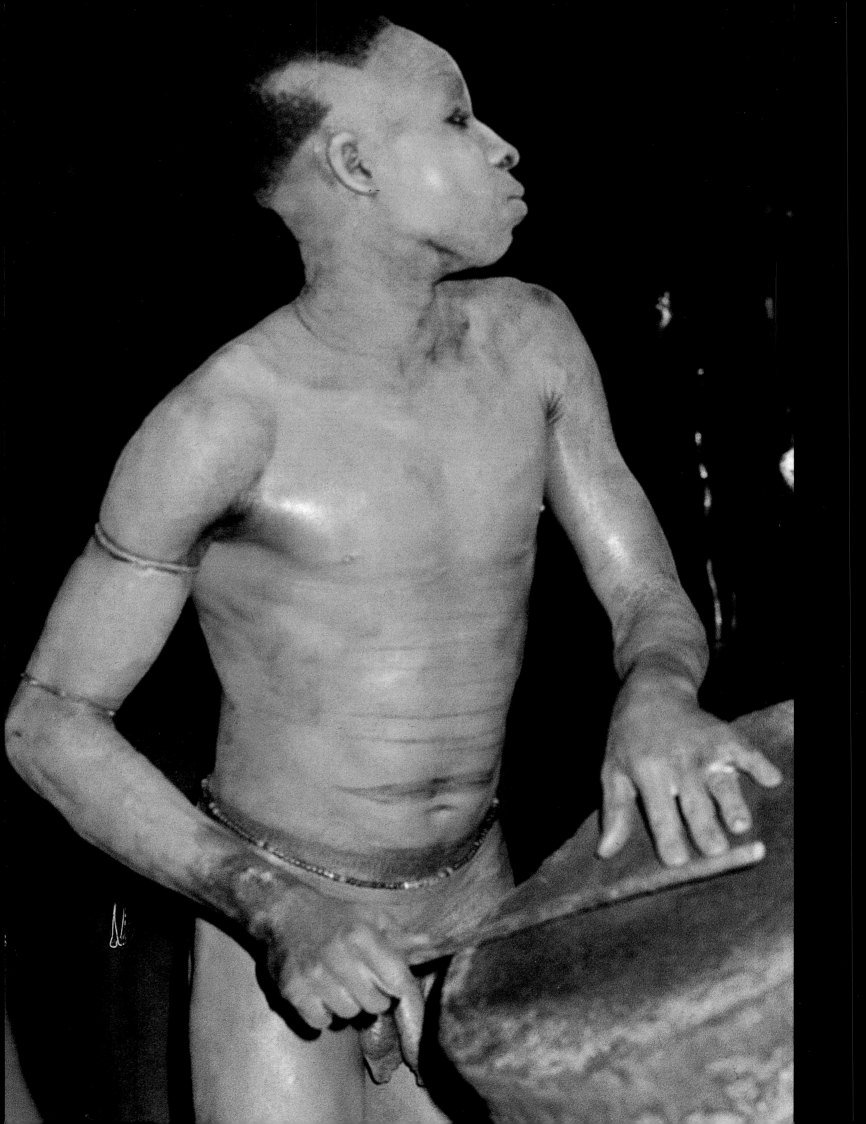

MAASAI

Maasai women preparing to move house. The Maasai call such settlements *engang* or *boma*. They are kraals of primitive huts covered with cow dung which serve as shelter for a few weeks. The Maasai, being nomads, have no fixed quarters. As soon as there is no grazing left they move on.

Maasai in front of their kraal. Kilimanjaro in the background.

Top left – A shepherd boy.
Bottom left – An elderly Maasai. The older men have great power and are highly respected by the warriors.
Right – A Maasai warrior, a *moran* in the Maasai language. These warriors almost always look distant and suspicious when faced with a stranger.

Maasai men consulting a *laibon*. The *laibon* is a high priest and the chief of a Maasai group. The Maasai believe that he has magic powers. He can be recognised by the white symbol on his forehead. He heaps stones of various colours on a cloth, and from this tells a Maasai what action to take.

Left – A young Maasai girl whose task it is to look after the small children.
Right – Young Maasai warriors attach great importance to their appearance. To appeal to the girls, this Maasai is painting a pattern on his face with a mixture of oil and crushed ochre rock.

Maasai with their herd. The cattle have been collected here to be bled. The Maasais', especially the Maasai warriors', favourite food is fresh cattle blood mixed, half and half, with milk. They believe this will give them great strength. The Maasai cattle are the epitome of their life and religion. The animals are sacred to them, and their favourite animal means more to them than their most beautiful wives.

Top left – Blood is taken from a cow. A tourniquet is applied to the carotid artery of the animal, and while a Maasai keeps a firm hold on the beast, a small opening is made in the artery with an arrow.
Bottom left – The blood is caught in a calabash. The wound is carefully closed so that the animal can be let out to graze again.
Right – A Maasai warrior with bead ornaments. It is typical of the Maasai that many of the toughest warriors have feminine facial features.

Left – This young Maasai warrior allowed himself to be photographed without protest, which was exceptional. He had an especially beautiful spear, the pride of every *moran*. As long as a warrior is carrying his spear he will not evade an attack, however dangerous. He trusts the strength of his weapon completely.
Right – The helmet hairstyle is made of red clay. This is a beauty treatment for the warrior's hair, since the clay, permeated with oil, makes the hair soft so that the long plaits are easier to braid. The hair and clay helmet is worn for ten to fourteen days.

When a Maasai becomes a warrior he arranges his hair elaborately. He lets it grow and braids it carefully into long, thin plaits. The warriors alone help one another, the women never arrange the warriors' hair. Fine woollen threads are braided into the hair to make it more attractive. The ends of the braids are bound with fine goat leather.

The warriors wear their hair plaited for nine years. After this their heads are shaved during an important ceremony. This is the most painful moment of their lives for many *morans*. It is the occasion when they cease to be warriors, leaving the caste which is the summit of the life of all male Maasai. They also mourn the loss of their beautiful hair. From now on they are just fathers of families and belong with the older people.

Maasai warrior with spears and shield.
The ball of trimmed ostrich feathers on the tip of the spear means that the Maasai comes in peace. The shields are made of buffalo skin. The decorations on the shield have different meanings and show to which group the Maasai warrior belongs. There are many subdivisions among the Maasai tribes. One can also see the degree of courage from the decorations on the shield. They show how many lions and rhino the warrior has killed.

A group of Maasai at the start of a lion hunt in Tanzania.
A lion has broken into the herd and taken a calf. The warriors will track the lion. A lion's mane, such as one of them is wearing, is given to a warrior when he kills a lion with his spear on his own without help.

Left – The expression of this warrior shows the characteristic qualities of the Maasai: pride, courage and fearlessness.
Right – The Maasai girls are as beautiful as the men. They have a great deal of freedom until they marry. They can take several lovers before marriage without loss of respect.

This Maasai looked at us very suspiciously. I was surprised when he fearlessly walked past a lion. When my driver, a Kikuyu noticed that I was apprehensive, he smiled and said, 'Maasai aren't afraid of lions, but lions are afraid of Maasai!' This was no joke, for the chief enemies of the lions are the Maasai. The lions' strongly developed sense of smell gives them warning of the Maasais' approach.

A Maasai warrior on a lion hunt in the open steppes of southern Tanzania. He is wearing a lion's mane trophy on his head.

The start of a Maasai ceremony.

Warriors and girls dancing during a ceremony.

Hundreds of Maasai get together for these great ceremonies. During the rhythmic dances which continue for hours, they work themselves up to such a pitch that many of them fall into a trance.

ANIMALS IN MAASAI TERRITORY

A gerenuk.

Top left – A group of lions.
Bottom left – A jackal watching approaching animals which might dispute its right to its prey.
Right – A lion in a tree, where it can sleep protected from its enemies.

Left – Portrait of a lion.
Top right – Jackals, vultures and marabous share the remains of a lion's meal.
Bottom right – A hyena keeping a sharp look-out.

A mother zebra with her young. These animals are especially in danger from lions.

Flamingoes at Lake Nakuru.

Rhinos in the Ngorongoro crater.

A cheetah hunting in the Serengeti. These big cats are the fastest animals in Africa. They can go at a speed of almost 100 km an hour.

A group of impala gazelles. The impalas are exceptionally strong jumpers. They can leap over a truck without the slightest difficulty.

It is almost impossible to imagine the landscape of East Africa without giraffes and umbrella thorns. The giraffes often live in large herds. I have counted as many as forty animals in a group. They use their hoofs to defend themselves against lions.

The most dangerous animal in Africa is the buffalo. Many an experienced hunter has been killed by one. They have enormous strength. Wounded, they may trample their adversary, which is usually man, to death and rip the body to pieces with their horns.

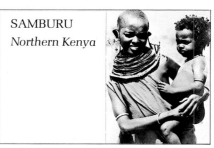

SAMBURU
Northern Kenya

The Samburu are related to the Maasai and like them are a pastoral people who live in northern Kenya. One of the Samburu's most striking features is the great number of bead necklaces the women and girls wear.

Left – Samburu youth.
Right – Samburu girl. The brass bangles on her arm show that she is engaged.

The elephant-hair necklaces the Samburu woman wears indicate the high regard the tribe has for her.

This beautiful Samburu girl was not at all shy of the camera.

Lake Manyara in Tanzania.

A still from *Black Cargo*, a film about the contemporary slave trade which was never completed. Shooting this scene was not without danger since hundreds of hippos were swimming about in the water, and the light boat, which we had built ourselves, might well have capsized. This photograph was taken on Lake Albert in Uganda.

Also from the film *Black Cargo*. We had to find strongly built actors for the parts of the slaves, and this was difficult in East Africa where the people are mostly tall and slim.

227

From the plane above Mount Kilimanjaro, its summit covered in new snow.

Falata nomads beside the White Nile. They are for ever on the move. They have to find suitable pasture and water for their enormous herds. These nomads are rich. The women, and even the children, wear gold and silver bangles on their arms and legs.

The Falata nomads pride themselves on breeding cattle with the most enormous horns.

An extended family often owns a herd of as many as a thousand cattle.

DINKA ·
MURLE · NUER

Southern Sudan

Nowadays one hardly ever sees Dinkas wearing their traditional bead belts. Thanks to their great intelligence they have integrated very quickly and are often important officials in the Sudanese government. Tall and slim, one can recognise them by the six horizontal lines tattooed on their foreheads. When I took this photograph it was the only time in Africa that my life was in danger from the local people.

Murle girls and women. This tribe lives in the east of the southern Sudan near the Ethiopian border. Strangers seldom visit the Murle since vehicles have to cross miles of swamp. It rains there for many months, and there are no bridges over the rivers.

All Murle girls and women wear head ornaments of blue beads. Since these ornaments are very heavy, they are held up by a leather band.

Murle women as well as men love to smoke hookahs. Though we were there for only a short time, everyone was welcoming and friendly to us.

A Nuer. Their foreheads are marked with decorative scars like those of the Dinkas. They bleach their hair with cow-dung. Their earrings are made of an ivory ring and plaited elephant and giraffe hair. The Nuer live in the swamplands south of Malakal with their cattle which they idolize as much as the Maasai do theirs.

The Latuko live in the south-eastern region of the Sudan. Unfortunately I was only able to stay with them for a few hours since Sudanese officers arrived to tell us that there had been a coup d'etat. It was April 1969 and President Numeiri came to power. The metal helmets of the Latuko are famous. They are lined with felt, and are skillfully made to measure for every Latuko warrior. These Latuko warriors are greatly feared for their strength and courage.

Steppe fire in the southern Sudan. Fire often breaks out spontaneously owing to the great heat and can rage for days, destroying all the trees on the large hilly tracts. This means that the people of the region sustain enormous losses since wood is their most important product. They need it to build their huts and to cook their food.

THE SHILLUK

Southern Sudan

The favourite son of the Shilluk king who died a few years ago. Of the many tribes who live in the southern Sudan, the Shilluk are one of the most interesting. Like the Maasai, Dinkas and Nuer, they belong to the Nilotes who came from Egypt as nomads in the past. They settled on the fertile banks of the Nile north-west of Malakal, becoming cattle breeders, fishermen and farmers. The Shilluk tribe numbers about one hundred thousand.

All the warriors of the Shilluk tribe wear wigs. These are made of animal hair and are knotted into their own hair. After a time the wig is exchanged for a new, larger one, and its place is finally taken by an even larger wig. The wigs are usually decorated with ostrich feathers.

To keep the shape of the wig intact, the Shilluk warriors sleep on a specially made wooden head support.

This Shilluk warrior looks like an Egyptian mummy.

All the Shilluk, not only the warriors but even the women and children, wear a tattoo on their forehead which looks like a string of beads. This is their tribal symbol. The warriors in the photograph have heightened the effect of the tattoo with white paint.

The cheerfulness of these Shilluk drummers is typical of the whole tribe. All the Shilluk I met were gentle and friendly and this constitutes a great contrast with their pronounced warlike skill.

This elderly Shilluk, seen here at the start of a ceremony in honour of the king, is wearing a wig made of monkey hair.

Almost all Shilluk warriors own large shields like these, skillfully made of crocodile leather. They are their most important defensive weapon in a fight.

The Shilluk king Kur dances at the head of his red-robed bodyguard and his warriors. The Shilluk are the only tribe in Africa which has been a monarchy since primeval times.

The king is the only Shilluk who looks well-fed. His tribe loves and honours him and he has 107 wives. But an old cruel tribal law decrees that he has to die when he is past the height of his powers. The Shilluk believe that a king whose powers are diminishing will bring misfortune to his people. During a feast the king is given a poisoned drink. He is then buried with great ceremony.

A Shilluk procession in honour of their king.

THE NUBIANS ·
MESAKIN

*Province of
Kordofan · Sudan*

More than half a million Nubians live in the province of Kordofan. Most of the Nubians have been westernized for decades. Only some of the Nubian tribes have isolated themselves, retreating into the Nuba Mountains in the south of the province of Kordofan. They are the poorest but also the happiest of the Nubians whom I came to know. This tribe has about ten thousand members. There are more than a hundred different Nubian tribes. Each has its own language.

Nubian settlements in the southern valleys of the Nuba Mountains.

229

On the way to the Nubians, A typical landscape of the Sudanese steppe where water is precious.

These trees bloom after the rainy season. It is inadvisable to touch the blossoms, for the whole tree is poisonous. Blossom, trunk and roots contain strychnine.

A Nubian girl in front of her house. A Nubian house is made up of five or six buildings around an inner courtyard. There is only one entrace to these houses which look like small fortresses and which, in the past, were easily defended against slave traders.

The Nubians are very musical. Every Nubian makes himself an instrument rather like a guitar and everyone plays their own tunes.

The expression of these two Nubian youths shows how good-natured the Mesakin Nubians are. They are very emotional and are the most peaceful of the African people, in contrast with the Nubians of Kau.

Nubian men harvesting dura. This provides 90% of the Nubians' food. This cereal is a cross between maize and corn and contains valuable minerals and vitamins.

The girls grind the dura on a stone.

A shepherds' camp which the Nubians call *noppo* and the Arabs *seribe*. The Nubians consider this a sacred place and no woman may enter it. During the dry months only the powerful pugilists live here with the young boys who look after the cattle and who have to keep up the camp fires.

The white ash with which the Mesakin Nubians cover themselves or paint white decorations on their bodies, has ritualistic significance. They believe that the white ash will give them strength, since it is a symbol of their religion.

The consecration ceremony of a youth, admitting him to the caste of the most powerful pugilists. This is a high point in the life of every young Nubian.

While ash is being rubbed into the young man's body, he is so overwhelmed by his feelings that he goes into a trance.

The inhabitants of a Nubian village set out for a pugilist festival. At the head are the four most powerful pugilists carrying the flags.

This is Nato, the greatest pugilist of Tadoro. He is the host at a big pugilist festival. The ornament he is holding, called *mare* by the Nubians, can only be worn during a fight by those pugilists who are considered almost invincible, since the heavy ornament of leather and brass rings is a great handicap for a fighter.

Before the start of the bout, the pugilists observe each other intently. They have great strength and skill. the one whose back first touches the ground is the loser.

The victor. He expresses his joy by dancing.

At the end of a pugilist fight, the groups from the various Nubian villages assemble and march, dancing and singing, to a place where they can all sit down and enjoy themselves deep into the night, drinking Marisse beer and singing. The parasols show that articles produced by industrial societies have found their way to the Nubians even in these distant valleys.

Some of the victors proudly wear English pith helmets. They have decorated them with strings of beads.

THE SOUTH-EASTERN NUBIANS

Nyaro · Kau · Fungor

An elderly Nubian with his drum, waiting for the start of a dance.

Part of the village of Fungor. It lies below an enormous rock. The south-eastern Nubians live about 200 km to the west of the Mesaki Nubians. Their language and customs are quite unlike those of the Mesakin, nor are they as poor as the Mesakin since they have more water and larger pastures. They are the artists among the Nubians. Their manner of painting their faces and bodies is unique. They have also stood out longest against the incursions of other ways of life. Their pride and courage resembles that of the Maasai.

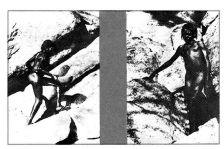

Left – A Nubian woman with a calabash. Since the houses are mostly built on stony ground, the road to them leads over rocks.
Right – Even the youngest girls rub themselves with oil every day. They mix the oil with ochre so that they are painted from top to toe. This gives them an exotic appearance.

These Nubians have killed a large leopard. The big cats often come at night into the Nubian villages, kill cattle and do a lot of damage. The Nubians set traps for them near the few watering places. When a leopard is caught it is killed with a gun shot. Only a few of the Nubians own old guns which they have inherited from their fathers who fought with the Sudanese and Egyptians against the Turks. The valuable leopard skin is sold to Arab traders.

The favourite occupation of young Nubian men who are called *kanudor*. is to improve their appearance. Their vanity is as great as their courage and valour. Each one of them uses his imagination and skill to paint himself in the most interesting possible ways.

This Nubian's mask is a fascinating artistic creation. All the colours, except the blue which the Nubians acquire by barter from the Arabs, are natural dyes which they make themselves.

A Nubian never repeats the lines and decorations of his mask. He paints himself a new face every day. His imagination is inexhaustible in inventing new patterns. The Nubians take special care with their hair-styles, spending hours of patient work, a friend helping, to produce a work of art, such as this.

A Nubian mask is hardly ever symmetrical. The Nubians tend to choose asymmetrical patterns, not only for their faces but also for their bodies. In spite of this, the decorations produce a harmonious effect.

This beautiful girl is from Kau. Her name is Haua and she was about twelve years old when the photograph was taken.

The south-eastern Nubians call their knife-fights zuar. All young men have to take part in them for about ten years after they are eighteen. It is not known whether there are other people in the world who practise such fights, using heavy, round double-bladed knives attached to their wrists. It is a very hard, but fair, sport.

Before the start of a dance in a village called Nyaro. The first girls have arrived. In their hands they carry long whips which are part of this ancient dance. The spectators are waiting on the surrounding rocks. A dance of this sort is called njertun by the Nubians. The word means love-dance.

The start of a love-dance in which only girls who have not slept with a man can take part. The virgins can choose a man they wish to marry on this particular day. The men, who wait to be chosen in the shadow of the straw roof, are all zuar fighters. The victors have, of course, a better chance with the girls.

Left – Two girls are standing in front of a man. Both girls are about to put their legs over the shoulders of the same man. If this happens, the decision rests with the man.

This Nubian is the hero of the day, since he has remained both unvanquished and uninjured. He has also attracted the attention of the girls by the special decorations on his back.

Here we see the girls standing in front of the men. This is the moment of the greatest tension among the men. They are not allowed to look at the girls, their eyes are fixed on the ground. They wear small bells on their ankles which are in constant movement. The girls wait for a drumroll which signals that they can lay their legs on the shoulders of the men they have chosen.

The dances, which become more and more frenzied, go on for hours – until the sun sets and dusk falls.

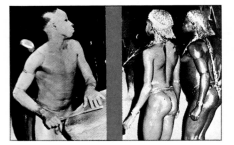

Some groups dance into the night.

A full moon above the rock-face of Kau.